Birth of Piglets

First published 1984
© Jane Miller 1984
All rights reserved

Set in 15 on 19 pt Itek Century Schoolbook by
Copyright Ltd, London
Printed & made in Great Britain by
W. S. Cowell Ltd, Ipswich, for
J. M. Dent & Sons Ltd
Aldine House, 33 Welbeck Street, London W1M 8LX

British Library Cataloguing in Publication Data

Miller, Jane
    Birth of piglets.
    1. Swine—Juvenile literature
    2. Parturition—Juvenile literature
    I. Title
    636.4'08984   SF395.5

    ISBN 0-460-06136-4

The author would like to thank the following for their invaluable help and assistance with this book:

J.R. Beacroft, farmer
David Mansbridge
David Buck
Lesley Foster
Alan Green
Steven Mutch
Dennis Brown

Birth of Piglets

Jane Miller

J.M. Dent & Sons Ltd
London & Melbourne

We all know what pigs look like, but not many of us have the chance of going to a pig farm to see for ourselves how they are born and reared. Pigs are farmed in different ways. Many are reared in indoor units. But this book is about outdoor pigs—those which are kept outside all year long.

The herd of over 600 sows grazes in 100 acres of rolling grassland, divided into paddocks by electric fences. Every year the herd is moved to fresh land which helps to keep the pigs healthy. The land grazed by them will have been well fertilized so it is ideal for growing cereal crops.

The sows—mother pigs—give birth to litters of piglets about every five months. There are usually at least ten piglets to a litter. Farmers raise pigs to produce the pork, bacon, ham, gammon, and sausages that we buy in the shops to eat. Over the years many different breeds of pig have been developed in order to produce the best meat. Certain companies specialize in breeding pure varieties of pigs which are then sold to farmers. The farmer whose animals appear in this book buys his pigs from a pig breeding company. The females are called Camborough Blues—a crossbreed of two pure varieties, Wessex Saddleback and British Landrace. On the farm these females will be mated with boars—male pigs, in this case a purebred variety known as Large Whites. So the piglets you see are very mixed indeed.

There are many different breeds of pigs just as there are many different races of human beings, but they all belong to the family called *suidae,* which comes from the Latin word for pig, *sus.* Similarly, human beings belong to a larger family, or order, known as primates which includes apes and monkeys. The order that pigs belong to is called *ungulata,* the scientific name for hoofed mammals.

A female pig is called a sow only after she has had her first litter of piglets. Before having their first litters female pigs are known as gilts. The sows you see here were born on another farm, coming to this one at the age of ten weeks.

These are gilts which have just arrived on the farm. Never before
having lived in the open they are first kept in the training paddock
while becoming used to their new surroundings. They must learn, too,
to stay inside the electric fence around the paddock. When they come
into season at 210 days (seven months) they will be ready to learn
about mating with boars, and then about having piglets.

This gilt is being driven to her paddock by Lesley, a stockman, who guides her using a pig-board. This is the correct way. Without a board the pig will run in a different direction.

Here is a gilt with her first piglets. Once she has raised the litter she will be known as a sow, and will start having another family.

The orange ear-tag that shows she is a gilt is being changed to the yellow tag of a sow.

Now she is having three nostril rings fitted into the gristle of her snout. Although this does hurt at first, pigs' snouts are tough. The rings are designed to stop them rooting up the land as they graze in the paddocks.

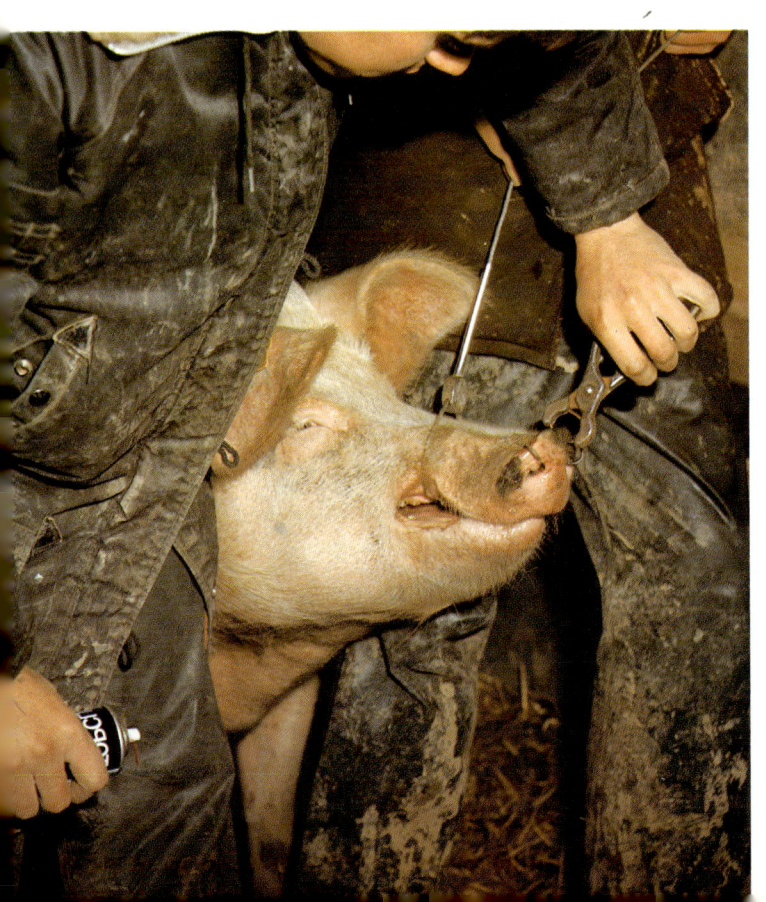

This is one of 30 Large White boars on this farm, with Steve, another of the stockmen. The boar is the father of many of the piglets you will see.

A sow has come into season, and the boar is mating with her. During mating he fertilizes the sow by passing his sperm into her body. This means that she will now be in-pig (or pregnant), and will give birth to piglets in three months, three weeks and three days— about 114 days after mating.

During the gestation period, the time when the piglets are growing inside their mothers, the sows live and graze together in the paddocks. They are cared for by the stockmen.

There are sow-huts in every paddock, and in these the sows sleep. The stockmen make sure that the pigs have lots of bedding straw, carting it to the huts on the tractor.

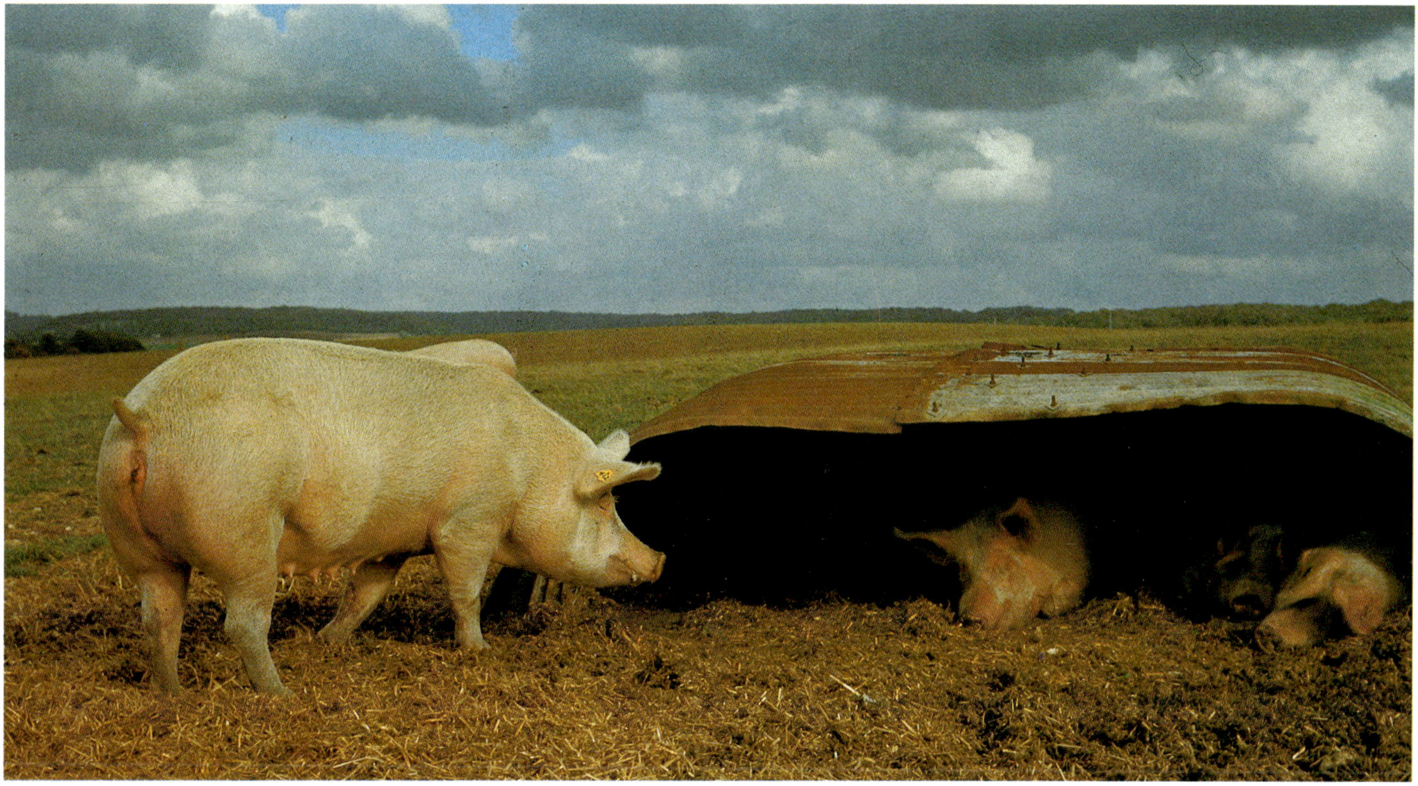

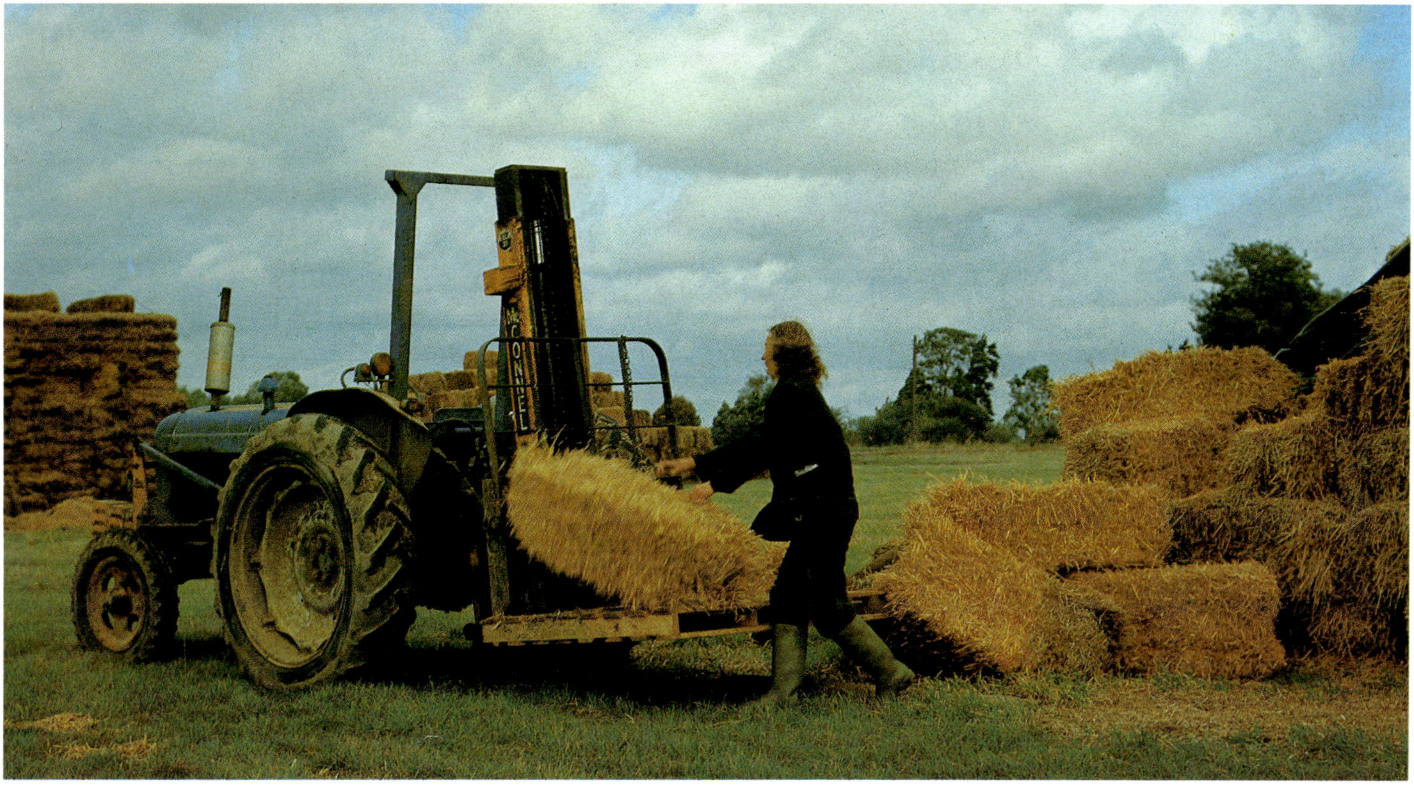

Every morning the sows are fed. The stockman takes round a huge feed trailer with tote-bins filled with blocks of pigmeal, known as sow-biscuits. Always hungry, the sows wait impatiently in the paddocks for the feed-trailer to arrive. Each sow is given about 3 kilos of sow-biscuits as a basic ration, but as much as 6 kilos when they have piglets to feed. In summer they need less because there is grass to eat in the paddocks.

Here is David, another stockman, pouring out the sow-biscuits from the tote-bin. He spreads them across the paddocks so that each sow receives her share.

Sows need to drink a great deal of water, as much as 2 gallons (9 litres) a day, and even more in summer when their piglets are suckling. If they do not have enough water they pant, becoming dehydrated, which means that their bodies lose water. They can easily suffer from sunstroke, too. While they drink from the troughs in their paddocks they deliberately spill water to make wallows, and then lie in the muddy pools to cool off. In very hot weather extra water has to be carted to keep the wallows filled.

Even in winter sows are always thirsty, and chew ice and snow for extra liquid. When the pipes to the troughs are frozen, the stockmen must cart water to all the paddocks.

Here the sows crowd together to drink from the troughs as Steve fills them by hose.

When the snow melts, or when it rains, the tracks become so muddy that it is difficult to drive the farm machinery around the paddocks.

The pig-trailer ploughs through the mud, while sows root for their sow-biscuits, churning up the ground with their snouts.

These sows are nearly ready to farrow which means they will give birth. You can see how large one has grown, and how her udder is swollen with milk ready for her piglets.

A few days before the sows are due to have their piglets, the stockmen load them into the pig-trailer and move them to the farrowing paddocks.

In each paddock there are ten farrowing huts spaced out in rows. Each hut is just large enough for a sow to lie down inside with her piglets. At the entrance is a nest-box which keeps the newborn piglets from roaming.

A sow watches David as he prepares the huts with dry straw bedding on which she will lie down to give birth.

When a sow knows she is ready to farrow she looks for a quiet place. Usually she will go inside a hut. This hut has a fox-light on the roof. Every farrowing paddock has one light like this. At night it flashes continuously, frightening away foxes which sometimes kill newborn piglets, while the sow is in the process of giving birth.

This sow is farrowing, and already several piglets have been born. They are born about every fifteen minutes over a period of several hours. A sow has many piglets, usually about ten, though sometimes as many as eighteen. But if she has too many not all will survive. The sow herself becomes exhausted during the births.

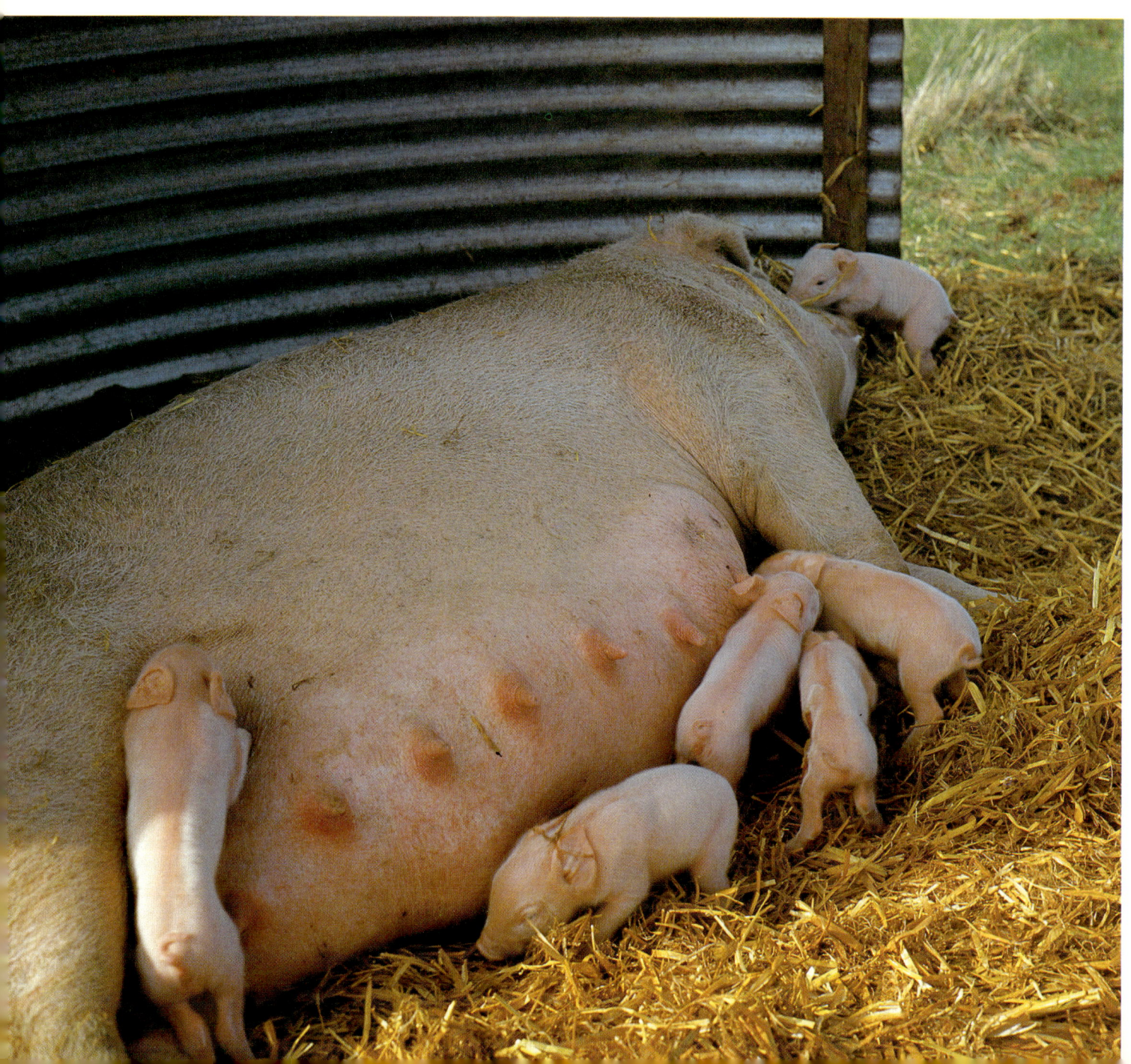

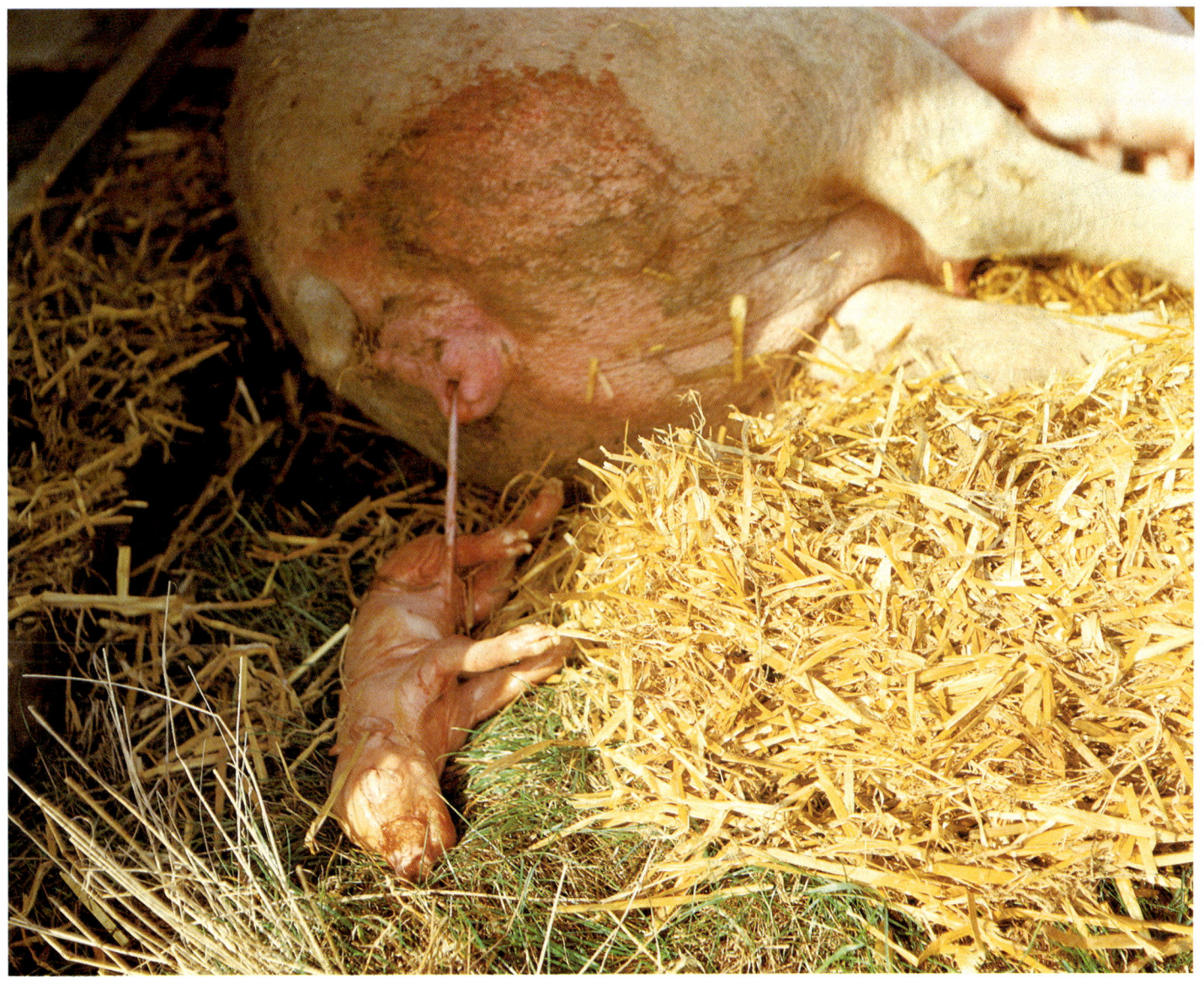

Each piglet emerges still attached to its mother by the umbilical cord.
It was through this cord that the piglet was fed while inside the sow.
You can see how perfectly formed the piglet is at birth.

Within minutes of its birth, the tiny piglet stands up. The one which has just been born moves round the huge body of its mother searching for her udder and milk. In doing so the cord will break and the piglet will be free. Unlike some animals the sow does not lick her piglets clean as they are born, nor does she nuzzle them. But it is amazing how quickly they find their way to her udder and learn to suckle while other piglets are being born.

The first milk the sow produces for her piglets is especially rich. It is called colostrum, and it gives the piglets a healthy start in life. At birth a piglet weighs about 1.35 kilos (3lbs), whereas the mother weighs about one hundred times as much—135 kilos (300 lbs). But although they are so tiny at first, the piglets grow rapidly.

With so many piglets born it is not surprising that the sow sometimes injures them. In the picture above you can see that one piglet is bleeding. This was caused by the sow accidentally treading on it.

This one is being revived by Steve because its mother has rolled on it by mistake.

Each morning and evening Steve, who is in charge of the farrowing sows, goes on his rounds inspecting the sows in the farrowing paddocks. Here he is tipping back a hut in order to check that all is well with a new litter. There are several things that have to be done soon after piglets are born.

First of all Steve sprays a red mark on the sow's neck to show that she has farrowed. Then he drives her away while he counts the piglets for the herd records.

Taking the piglets one by one, Steve holds them firmly by the head, snipping off the 8 sharp eye-teeth with which each one is born. This is done so that when the piglets suckle they do not make the sow's udder sore, or injure each other while suckling. Steve uses special teeth clippers.

Next, holding each piglet by a back leg—the correct way—Steve gives them all two injections, one of iron and the other of antibiotics, to keep them fit and to help them grow strong.

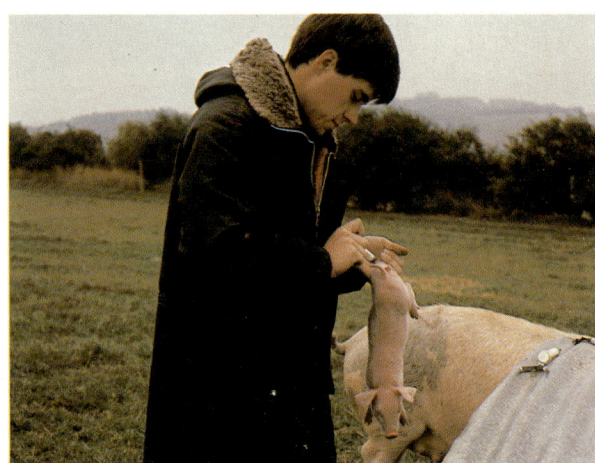

Then he snips off part of each piglet's tail. This is necessary because they sometimes chew each other's tails.

Having done all this Steve allows the anxious sow to return to her piglets.

These small piglets are only a few days old. They are in their nest-box enjoying the warm sun.

Piglets in a litter tend to do things all at the same time, sleeping, waking and suckling. They grow so quickly that they are soon able to follow their mother outside the hut and to go for walks around the paddock.

A sow knows when her piglets are hungry and lies down to feed them. The piglets climb all over her, greedily searching for her teats, squealing and pushing each other out of the way. When the sow decides that the piglets have had enough milk she heaves herself up and the piglets roll off into the grass.

As they grow bigger the piglets become more and more demanding. Sometimes they suckle their mother when she is standing in the paddock, climbing over one another to reach her teats. They even grab at her teats as she is walking along. Piglets seem always to be squealing noisily for milk.

Becoming independent, the piglets will roam quite a long way from their mother. Often they race about the paddock together, squealing, sometimes joining other litters doing the same thing.

But when they are tired or hungry somehow they manage to sort themselves out and to return to their own mothers.

Nearly always there are one or two piglets which are smaller than the rest of the litter. These are known as runts. Once the majority of the litter is ready to be weaned from their mother the runts are put into a special weaner-hut like the one in this picture. These runts are too small to go off with the other stronger piglets to continue their rearing. They sleep inside the hut, coming out on to the platform for their food and water.

The runts now have to learn to manage without their mother's milk, and to nibble creep feed, tiny pellets of dried milk, sugar and cereals. They discover how to raise the lids of the feed hoppers with their snouts, and to suck water, which has antibiotics added to it, from nipples on a tank.

When they first come to the weaner-hut, the piglets are usually weak, so Lesley needs to give them special care.

She injects them with vitamins and antibiotics. Within a few days the runts have grown used to living in the weaner-hut. Once they are large enough they will join the other piglets on the rearing farm.

Litters of piglets are ready to be weaned when they weigh about 5½ kilos (12 lbs) at the age of three weeks. The stockmen collect them from their huts early in the morning. First the sow is moved out, then the pig-board is placed across the entrance to the hut to prevent the piglets from running into the paddock. The piglets from each hut are then loaded into the pig-trailer.

Finally the stockmen have made the rounds of all the huts and the pig-trailer is full of young weaners. Now they go off to another farm for the next stage of their rearing.